Gearhead Garage

TOP FUEL DRAGSTERS

DEANNA CASWELL

WORLD BOOK

This World Book edition of *Top Fuel Dragsters* is published by agreement between Black Rabbit Books and World Book, Inc. © 2018 Black Rabbit Books, 2140 Howard Dr. West, North Mankato, MN 56003 U.S.A. World Book, Inc., 180 North LaSalle St., Suite 900, Chicago, IL 60601 U.S.A.

Marysa Storm, editor; Grant Gould, interior designer; Michael Sellner, cover designer; Omay Ayres, photo researcher

Library of Congress Control Number: 2016049948

ISBN: 978-0-7166-9308-6

Printed in the United States at CG Book Printers, North Mankato, Minnesota, 56003. 3/17

Image Credits

Alamy: Tony Watson, 12–13; Wacky Racing / picturesbyrob, 9 (engine), 23; ZUMA Press, Inc., 8–9, 14–15, 18 (top), 24, 29 (Kalitta); AP Images: Jeff Speer / SPTSW, 4–5; dickkraft.com: Unknown, 11; https://www.cokertire.com: Tommy Lee Byrd, 20–21 (tires); http:www.motorsport.com: Action Sports Photography, 20–21; Getty Images: Bob Harmeyer, 27; David Goddard, 17; Leo Mason/Popperfoto, 31; Newscom: Jeff Spear, Cover; Sam Morris/Icon SMI 127, 29; Shutterstock: Ati design, 18 (bottom); Castleski, 28 (bottom); Digital Storm, 3; Ken Tannenbaum, 29 (bottom); Michael Stokes, 1, 6, Back Cover; nitinut380, 22; Philip Rubino, 32; Wikrom Kitsamritchai, 7, 28–29 (timeline dragster) Every effort has been made to contact copyright holders for material reproduced in this book. Any omissions will be rectified in subsequent printings if notice is given to the publisher.

CONTENTS

CHAPTER 1

Raw

The Top Fuel (TF) **dragster** rockets down the track. Flames shoot out from the sides. The ground shakes. **G-forces** pin the driver's body to the seat. The dragster reaches 330 miles (531 kilometers) per hour. Then, parachutes pop open. The car slows to a stop.

Fast and Fun

TF cars are built for short bursts of high speed. In fact, they are the fastest-**accelerating** cars ever. TF races finish just seconds after they begin.

TF cars speed up faster than jets. They take off with more force than rockets.

By the Numbers

less than .8 SECOND

TIME TO GO FROM 0 to 100 MILES (161 KM) PER HOUR

25 FEET (8 METERS)
length of a TF car

LESS THAN 5 SECONDS

HOW LONG A TF RACE LASTS

AROUND
10,000
**AMOUNT OF HORSEPOWER
IN A TF ENGINE**

ABOUT
2,320
POUNDS
(1,052 kilograms)

**WEIGHT OF A TF
CAR WITH DRIVER**

1,000 FEET
(305 M)
TF race length

CHAPTER 2

The History of Top Fuel

Dragsters

By 1950, **drag racing** had become popular in the United States. Racer Dick Kraft wanted to race a lighter car. He took an old car and **stripped** it down. The car's lighter weight made it faster. It sped up quicker. It was ugly, but it won races.

Soon, people began building cars just for drag racing. These cars became light and powerful.

Kraft named his car "The Bug." Some people call it the first dragster.

Danger and Design

People called early TF cars slingshots. Drivers sat behind the engines. Engines were often pushed to their limits. Explosions were common. Blowups that happened right in front of drivers were very dangerous.

In 1970, driver Don Garlits lost half of a foot in an explosion. So he made a car with an engine in the back. With the new design, he won races and broke records. Now, all TF cars have rear engines.

PARTS OF A TOP FUEL DRAGSTER

SUPERCHARGER

FRONT WING

ENGINE

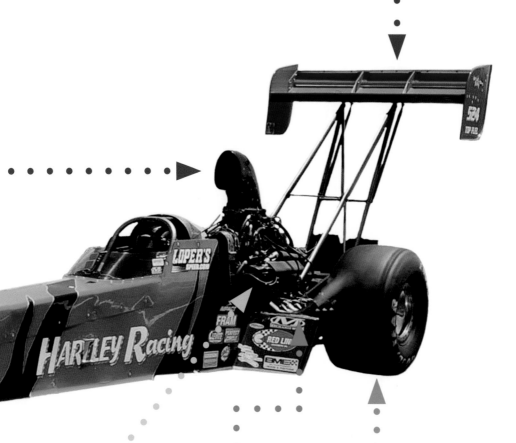

REAR WING

REAR SLICKS

EXHAUST PIPES

A Worldwide Sport

Drag racing began in California. Today, almost every U.S. state has tracks. Many other countries have TF racing too. The United Kingdom has the Santa Pod Raceway. It is considered the most popular track outside the United States.

During a race, all of a TF car's fuel isn't burned. The unburned fuel goes out the exhaust pipes. The pipes' heat **ignites** the fuel. Flames then come out of the pipes.

CHAPTER 3

Reaching Top Speeds

TF dragsters don't use gas. They run on **nitromethane**. It is called nitro for short. Nitro is called the "top fuel." The cars get their name from the fuel.

Nitro is different from everyday car fuel. It needs less oxygen to burn than gas. It also makes more power.

HOW FAST DO THEY GO?

In 2012, David Grubnic ran a TF race in 3.85 seconds. Here's how his race would have looked by the second on this track.

At **3.85** seconds,
HE WAS GOING 315 MILES
(507 KM) PER HOUR
AND HAD TRAVELED 1,000 FEET (305 M).

At **3** seconds,
HE WAS GOING 275 MILES
(443 KM) PER HOUR
AND HAD TRAVELED 650 FEET (198 M).

At **2** seconds,
HE WAS GOING 213 MILES
(343 KM) PER HOUR
AND HAD TRAVELED 231 FEET (70 M).

At **1** second,
HE WAS GOING 113 MILES
(182 KM) PER HOUR
AND HAD TRAVELED 75 FEET (23 M).

Sticky Slicks

TF rear tires are smooth rubber. The rubber sticks to the track. At the beginning of a race, the tires wrinkle and stretch. The tires' flexibility keeps them from losing **traction**. At the speeds TF cars go, the tires last only 2 miles (3 km).

Comparing Tires

TOP FUEL REAR TIRE

around 17 inches
(43 centimeters) wide

2-mile (3-km) life span

AVERAGE CAR TIRE

8.5 to 9.3 inches
(22 to 24 cm) wide

50,000-mile (80,467-km) life span

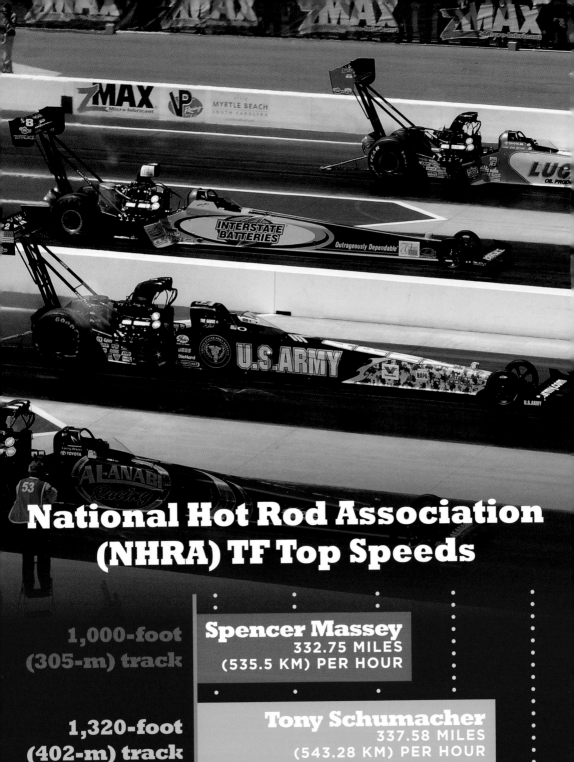

National Hot Rod Association (NHRA) TF Top Speeds

| 1,000-foot (305-m) track | **Spencer Massey** 332.75 MILES (535.5 KM) PER HOUR |
| 1,320-foot (402-m) track | **Tony Schumacher** 337.58 MILES (543.28 KM) PER HOUR |

CHAPTER 4

The Future of Top Fuel Dragsters

TF cars are still changing. Racing rules are too.

In 2008, driver Scott Kalitta died in a race. People realized they needed to make racing safer. Officials shortened TF races from 1,320 feet to 1,000 feet (402 m to 305 m). The leftover track gives cars more stopping room. There is less time to build speed. But cars still reach high speeds.

Top Fuel Technology

For years, TF cars were computer free. TF racing rules said devices could track information and speed. But technology could not help drive. In 2004, the NHRA approved **digital** controls. These controls make racing safer.

TF cars and racing have changed a lot over the years. No one knows what will be added or changed next. But one thing is certain. These cars will continue to be fast and exciting.

1971

Don Garlits switches to rear engine.

1950

Dick Kraft makes "The Bug."

1940

World War II ends.

1945

The first people walk on the moon.

1969

1999

Tony Schumacher becomes the first TF driver to reach more than 330 miles (531 km) per hour.

2008

Scott Kalitta dies.

2015

Spencer Massey sets speed record.

2016

The Mount St. Helens volcano erupts.

1980

Terrorists attack the World Trade Center and Pentagon.

2001

accelerate (ak-SEL-uh-reyt)—to gain speed

digital (DIJ-i-tuhl)—using computer technology

drag race (DRAYG RAYS)—a contest where people race cars at very high speeds over a short distance

dragster (DRAYG-ster)—a car that is made for drag racing

g-force (JEE-FOHRS)—the force of gravity or acceleration on a body

horsepower (HORS-pow-uhr)—a unit used to measure the power of engines

ignite (ig-NAHYT)—to catch fire

nitromethane (ny-tro-MEH-thayn)—a liquid fuel for rockets and high-performance engines

strip (STRIP)—to remove unimportant material

supercharger (SOO-pur-char-jur)—a device that brings in more air to an engine

traction (TRAK-shuhn)—the force that causes a moving thing to stick against the surface it is moving along

BOOKS

Caswell, Deanna. *Funny Cars.* Gearhead Garage. Mankato, MN: Black Rabbit Books, 2018.

MacArthur, Collin. *Inside a Drag Racer.* Life in the Fast Lane. New York: Cavendish Square, 2015.

Monnig, Alex. *Behind the Wheel of a Dragster.* In the Driver's Seat. Mankato, MN: Child's World, 2016.

WEBSITES

Basics of Drag Racing
www.nhra.com/nhra101/basics.aspx

Drag Racing Classes
www.nhra.com/nhra101/classes.aspx

How a Top Fuel Dragster Works
www.youtube.com/watch?v=-VF0JwxQqcA

INDEX